Knoxville, Tennessee

Knoxville, Tennessee

BY NIKKI GIOVANNI

illustrated by Larry Johnson

SCHOLASTIC INC.
New York

Giovanni, Nikki.
Knoxville, Tennessee / by Nikki Giovanni : illustrations by Larry Johnson.
        p.   cm.
Summary: Describes the joys of summer spent with family in Knoxville: eating
vegetables right from the garden, going to church picnics, and walking in the
mountains.
ISBN 0-590-47074-4
1. Afro-Americans — Tennessee — Knoxville — Social life and customs —
Juvenile poetry.   2. Family — Tennessee — Knoxville — Juvenile poetry.
3. Knoxville (Tenn.) — Juvenile poetry.   4. Children's poetry, American.
5. Summer — Juvenile poetry.   [1. Afro-Americans — Poetry.   2. Family life —
Poetry.   3. Knoxville (Tenn.) — Poetry.   4. Summer — Poetry.   5. American
poetry — Afro-American authors.]   I. Johnson, Larry, 1949–   Ill.   II. Title.
PS3557.I55K66   1994
811'.54 — dc20   93-8877
                                                                         CIP
                                                                         AC

Grateful acknowledgment is made to William Morrow and Company, Inc. for
permission to reprint "Knoxville, Tennessee" from *Black Feeling, Black Talk, Black
Judgement* by Nikki Giovanni, copyright © 1968, 1970 by Nikki Giovanni.

12 11 10 9 8 7 6 5 4 3 2   4 5 6 7 8 9/9

Printed in the U.S.A.   37

First Scholastic printing, February 1994

Book design by Adrienne M. Syphrett

I always like summer best

you can eat fresh corn

from daddy's garden

and okra
and greens
and cabbage

and lots of
barbecue
and buttermilk

and homemade ice-cream

at the church picnic

and listen to
gospel music
outside

at the church
homecoming

and go to the mountains with
your grandmother

and go barefooted

and be warm

all the time
not only when you go to bed

and sleep